HOLIDAY FUN

HALLOWEEN

KIM THOMPSON

NORWOOD HOUSE PRESS

Cataloging-in-Publication Data

Names: Thompson, Kim.
Title: Halloween / Kim Thompson.
Description: Buffalo, NY : Norwood House Press, 2027. | Series: Holiday fun | Includes glossary and index.
Identifiers: ISBN 9781978580626 (pbk.) | ISBN 9781978580633 (library bound) | ISBN 9781978580640 (ebook)
Subjects: LCSH: Halloween--Juvenile literature.
Classification: LCC GT4965.T548 2027 | DDC 394.2646--dc23

Published in 2027 by
Norwood House Press
2544 Clinton Street
Buffalo, NY 14224

Designer: Rhea Magaro
Editor: Tricia Hoffman

Photo credits: Cover, p. 1 Alexander Raths/Shutterstock.com; pp. 5, 21 FamVeld/Shutterstock.com; p. 7 Photo Spirit/Shutterstock.com; p. 8 Yuliia Markova/Shutterstock.com; p. 10 Wirestock Creators/Shutterstock.com; p. 11 Savicic/Shutterstock.com; p. 12 Kiselev Andrey Valerevich/Shutterstock.com; p. 13 Joseba Abenojar/Shutterstock.com; p. 14 Cory Seamer/Shutterstock.com; p. 15 Merydolla/Shutterstock.com; p. 16 Sean Locke Photography/Shutterstock.com; p. 17 Jaclyn Vernace/Shutterstock.com; p. 18 Tijana Moraca/Shutterstock.com; p. 19 Krakenimages.com/Shutterstock.com;

Printed in the United States of America

TABLE OF CONTENTS

HALLOWEEN IS HERE!

Leaves crunch under your feet. A ghost passes you on the sidewalk. It says, "Boo!"

On this **holiday**, it is fun to be a little scared. It is Halloween!

A SPECIAL DAY

Halloween comes every **autumn**.

It is always on October 31st.

Orange and black are the colors of Halloween. Orange is for fall leaves. Black may stand for the “death” of summer.

Halloween started thousands of years ago. People thought the **spirits** of dead people roamed Earth on this night.

People tried to trick the spirits by wearing costumes!

HOW TO CELEBRATE

People get out **spooky** decorations. There are witches, **zombies**, and monsters.

Some people go to **haunted** houses.

They are not really haunted!

Hayrides take people to pumpkin patches.

Pumpkins turn into **jack-o'-lanterns**!

There are fun parties. People bob for apples.

Kids choose costumes. Adults stock up on candy!

On Halloween night, people put on costumes. It is time to go out into the night. Kids knock on doors. They say, "**Trick or treat**!"

There are hardly any tricks. There are lots of treats!

On Halloween, people enjoy one scary night.

Everyone is dressed up, and everyone is happy!

GLOSSARY

autumn (AW-tuhm): the season between summer and winter; fall

haunted (HAWN-tid): visited by ghosts and other scary characters

holiday (HAH-li-day): a special day; a day when most people do not go to school or work because of a religious or national celebration

jack-o'-lanterns (JAK-uh-lan-turnz): hollowed-out pumpkins with faces carved into them and candles or lights put inside

spirits (SPIR-its): ghosts or other supernatural characters

spooky (SPOO-kee): strange or scary

trick or treat (trik or treet): words children say to ask for candy when they go from door to door on Halloween

zombies (ZAHM-beez): characters that look like dead bodies that have come back to life

THINKING QUESTIONS

1. When is Halloween?
2. What are the colors of Halloween? Why?
3. What are jack-o'-lanterns?
4. What does it mean to bob for apples?
5. Why do people wear costumes on Halloween?

INDEX

ABOUT THE AUTHOR

Kim Thompson lives in Columbus, Ohio, with her husband and two funny cats. She has written many books for kids. Her favorite Halloween candy is peanut butter cups. Her favorite holiday is the one that is coming up next!